My
Hope
Within
syllables

© Alta H Haffner 2024

ISBN: 9780796168672

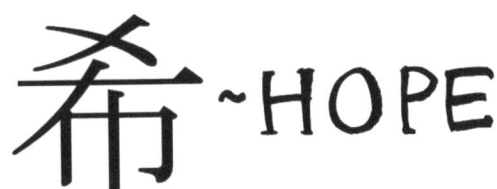

~HOPE

# About the book

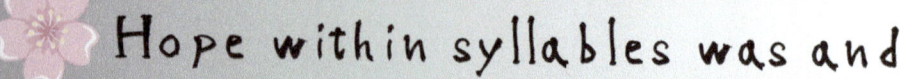

Hope within syllables was and

always will be my "soul child".

When I wrote my 1st ever

Haiku, I knew that I would be

counting syllables until my last

breath.

This book is a little sad but

incredibly hopeful.

# About the author

Alta H. Haffner is a Haiku poet whose work captures the essence of precious, fleeting moments with simplicity and depth. Born with a deep appreciation for the beauty of brevity, Alta's Haiku poems reflect her keen observation of nature and her ability to evoke emotions in just a few short lines.

Drawing inspiration from the ever changing seasons, the delicate balance of the natural world, and the quiet whispers of every new dawn, Alta's Haiku poems invite readers to slow down, pause, and appreciate the present moment. With a handful of syllables, she allows her readers to contemplate.

Through her Haiku poetry, Alta H. Haffner reminds us of the beauty that can be found in simplicity, the power of mindfulness, and the importance of being fully present in each moment.

your inner beauty
reflecting a sunny day
in midst of winter

do you remember
a touch silky soft and warm
leaning against thorns

strength of a woman
tears turned to titanium
rise to a new morn'

our misguided trust
such painful disappointments
truth hidden rainbow

lonely starry nights
forgotten promise at night
the sun beaming bright

my evergreen view
I cried a river of tears
you held icy snow

touch my scarlet lips
a sorrowful encounter
red spider lily

a gust of ume
japanese garden of hope
our sweet honey gone

ume- apricot blossoms

withered winter songs
our love bloomed at harvest moon
soon the morning chill

frosted emotions
fire warming the night chill
lullaby slumber

thoughts swept in chaos
the stars surrender to sun
lanterns have died now

blow dandelions
field of cold scattered wishes
a heart full of hope

bright hues still linger
kaleidoscope reflecting
peace from a distance

icy green forest
droplets collide into mud
in the dark of night

dandelion fluff
a breezy dance of wild weeds
scattering wishes

a purple wild haze
labyrinth of emotions
slowly fading now

curved cotton dreams fall
a view of a starry night
the moonlight hiding

trapped in our bubble
dancing in a sea of pain
exhaling to drown

frozen pinecone rise
greetings to the melted snow
sun in horizon

our shipwreck capsized
wild stark savage crow lurking
hyenas sly snark

glistening droplets
crimson rosebud opening
winter melted quick

memories fading
only darkest pain persists
bloody tears on page

waves on sandy shore
closer yet further away
pick up pretty shells

cast in ocean deep
yesterday you still loved me
memories buried

# TANKA

gentle with my heart
oh future lover of mine
fragile dreams of love

I have a cynical soul
and a romantic heartbeat

a sakura breeze
hold this dreaded pain for me
waterfall of tears

Sakura - Cherry blossom

cold dark words uttered
my veins frozen to your touch
disconnected souls

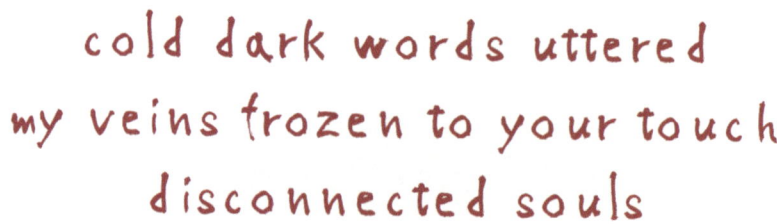

my cold lips trembling
confusion of rejection
icy emotions

night turns to yellow
sunflower greetings at morn
lonely tears smudged cheek

希

I watched him say bye
with every cold distant word
quietly faded

burning love letters
I cry because you mattered
crashing silently

agonizing heart
lonely unbearable thoughts
dull three letter words

grey dark skies above
speckled azure of hope now
because you live there

# TANKA

thoughts and memories
as the bright night light expands
I await the moon

through paths of pink sakura
voice echos forevermore

I need you to rest
the tears streaming down my face
do not let me lose

count your great blessings
for in the blink of an eye
it can fade away

moments of laughter
memory of hurt and pain
rose petals at dawn

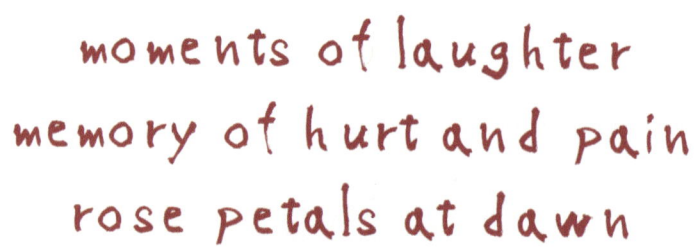

lingering snowfall
muddy road where nothing grows
heavy thunder clouds

windy hazy dusk
tranquility of moonlight
stormy horizon

希

soul no longer seek
I now have a breeze of hope
your memory lives

glorious new dawn
birds chirping for attention
still asleep with moon

希

an amber nightfall
my heart full of pensive thoughts
dusk to dawn feelings

a new dawn today
unconditional love gone
reflecting love now

hold you in my heart
forevermore love to hold
at dusk I will weep

only memory
seeking your face every day
only lonely thoughts

希

a low hazy moon
the night sounds speak to my soul
awaiting morn' clouds

path of fallen leaves
birds in flight before storm clouds
no sunny skies here

rain falling softly
pitter patter on window
dreamingly sleepy

lazy day, ponder
memories of you linger
memories fading

in your eyes I see
a river of memories
memories for now

a breath of winter
chill in my veins icy road
traveled since the dawn

icy heart of snow
dancing in yesterday's rain
tears embrace my soul

don't live in the past
you don't live there anymore
bright new beginnings

the calm of sunset
unwillingly surrender
an evening solace

the first dawn shining
glowing amber horizons
cosmos dancing slow

the moon my shadow
hiding my darkness within
a new dawn arise

tranquil sounds tonight
mesmerized and ancient thoughts
a new dawn of hope

a plum blossom greets
infinite beauty in morn'
while birds sit and wait

a sunflower smile
on this windy sunny day
with hope of some rain

pretty butterfly
contemplating in the sun
waiting for the rain

as the night darkens
lonely heart weeps at stars
the sun smiled brightly

flower petals dance
brightest colorful greetings
a storm full of dust

In the morning light
Happy birds sing their duets
The owl sleeps and dream

A willow tree weeps for rain
The thirsty brown leaves frowning

A thunderous storm
Soaking up the desert sand
Frogs leaping in ponds

leaves falling so slow
every white petal muddy
evergreen grasslands

windy jasmine breeze
hopes of forever, whispered
silent tear ~ escape

embrace each moment
with tender thoughts and your soul
bleeding heart on page

you find a way to
sneak in briefly, tenderly
again, fading slow

希

covered icy snow
the pastel pink sakura
a thick blanket folds

my voice of love, speaks
waiting for your soul, seeking
find me under, stars

full moon between clouds
the darkness all around me
awaiting the sun

a silent night sky
sound of bagpipes feintly heard
amazing grace ~Pray

希

amber leaves falling
a path to new beginnings
breathe in the morn' breeze

I'm dancing in hope
while watching amber sunsets
the starry sky greets

foggy magic morn'
a reflection to breathe in
hope and love collide

frozen statue now
no dancing dandelion
an elusive warmth

希

sun igniting day
a mineral aftertaste
soft waves shimmering

I'm alone again
you made your choice, just for you
look to sakura

sunflowers watching
starving tiny insects feast
On yesterday's weeds

a lilac blanket
a peaceful embrace of calm
Perfect harmony

forlorn memories
dark breezy cold winter's night
roaring crackling blaze

grey clouds hanging low
foamy waves crashing faster
an empty seashell

sakura petals
earth awaiting your caress
soft cold rain drizzling

view from my window
wind weaving and clouds darkened
silenced by thunder

希

sunset lullaby
hues of amber and crimson
a peaceful slumber

pensive winter thoughts
japanese instruments play
soul yearn to be free

soaking up soul words
all seventeen syllables
breathing, exhaling

your soul shines brightly
breath of sakura blossoms
breathing in and out

希

dramatic painful
heartache at the midnight moon
turn at the crossroad

lonely butterfly
searching now, forevermore
rest along the way

feel the breeze within
inhale sakura blessings
take the soul journey

rushing through my days
yearning for my dark solace
to nourish my soul

within syllables
Nozomu is what I have
hope forevermore

Nozomu - Hope

Aisuru, love live
be awakened with true love
soul everlasting

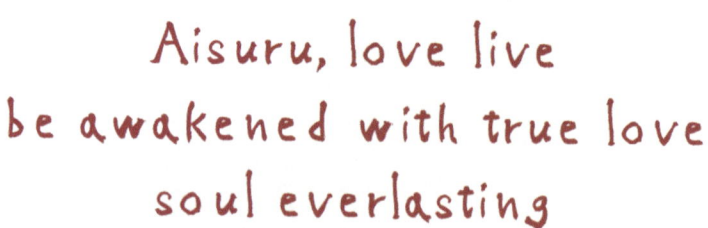

Assure- to cherish

only speak your truth
do not relate to darkness
your soul breathe again

much has changed for me
lonely but not alone now
and hope still lingers

希

tap tap tap tap tap
emotional freedom now
dusk to dawn healed soul

I soak it all up
seventeen syllables rest
sinking autumn sun

www.ingramcontent.com/pod-product-compliance
Lightning Source LLC
Chambersburg PA
CBHW042044290426
44109CB00001B/23